The Great Glen

The Great Glen was formed by ancient earth movements that wrenched and slid the crust sideways, forming a fault line running from coast to coast. Later glacial action was to further dramatise the scenery and add to the fierce beauty of this glen that runs coast to coast, from the deep-water anchorages of Loch Linnhe in the west to the salty tang of the Moray Firth. The nature of this geological upheaval can be imagined by considering that Foyers, a pleasing village on the quieter eastern side of Loch Ness has the same kind of ancient granite as Strontian, over sixty miles to the south-west, away from the Great Glen, tucked amongst the Hills of Ardgour. The mechanisms

through which this crustal movement took place need not concern the visitor today – though the occasional and most minor of earth tremors are still recorded – instead, a journey up the Great Glen is a rewarding experience for its sheer variety and beauty of the landscape and for the part the Great Glen has played in the

Right: *Looking across Loch Linnhe to Ben Nevis with Fort William below.* Below: *A romantic interpretation of the Moray Firth and Fort George*

history of the nation of Scotland and its communications from coast to coast both in peace and war. It was along this dividing line between Central and Northern Highlands that several important clans – Campbell, MacDonald, Stewart, Fraser – held their territories and fought their bloody battles. Not long after, the Great Glen was a natural route for General Wade and his road-

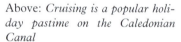

Above: *Cruising is a popular holiday pastime on the Caledonian Canal*

building programme, designed to further subdue the troublesome northern lands. Then the canal-builders came and joined the coasts by a magnificent waterway, still in use today. The Great Glen even saw the rise and fall of a sad little railway that, in its closing, was the earliest casualty in the vast contraction of Scotland's branch-line network.

With its broad sweep of hill-slope on either hand and good modern road network, the visitor by car is tempted to rush ever onwards. Fort William and Inverness are less than two hours apart. But it is better to slow down, seek out the byways and discover a little about the greatest – in distance and variety – of Scotland's glens.

Left: *The impressive Great Glen runs from coast to coast*

Loch Linnhe

For the best appreciation of the maritime landscape presented by the southern end of the Great Glen, it is best to start at Port Appin. Thousands of visitors don't, of course – hurrying instead between Oban and Fort William, content with their first views of Loch Linnhe from a layby on the main road. From Port Appin, the ferry leaves for Lismore, lying low-backed out in the sea-loch. But just out of sight and reached on foot from the ferry car park is evidence of the dramatic geological history of the area – an ancient arch in a stranded cliff, once formed by the sea but now raised and grassy beyond the

Right: The Ballachulish Bridge spans the narrows of Loch Leven at the south end of the Great Glen. Below: Castle Stalker with Ardgour beyond

reach of the tides.

Back towards the main road lies Castle Stalker, said to have once been the hunting lodge of James IV. This restored sixteenth-century tower stands privately on its own offshore islet. Beyond it and across Loch Linnhe, there are fine views northwards to the Ardgour Hills, which continue to

present a pleasing picture all the way to the Ballachulish Bridge. This fine bridge, opened since the mid-seventies, removed at a stroke the long summer ferry queues. Nearby Ballachulish was once the site of extensive slate quarrying, recalled now in an exhibition in the local tourist information centre.

New bridges in the north of Scotland have considerably reduced the numbers of small car-ferries still operating. North of Ballachulish on the Fort William Road the Corran Ferry still faithfully crosses the Corran Narrows, shortening the drive for visitors bound for the far west and Ardnamurchan. The main road continues speedily northwards, through pleasing mixed woods with patrolling buzzards, oyster-catchers on the shore and with forestry activities the main influence on the landscape.

Above: Evening motorists will catch spectacular sunsets from the roadside by Loch Linnhe

Below: The Corran Ferry shortens the journey to the Ardgour peninsula and far-western Ardnamurchan

Fort William

In season, Fort William looks into its own main street, as if attending to its own commercial businesses and keeping its back turned to the wealth of splendid scenery which surrounds it. Little or nothing remains of its military origins. Founded in 1690 and named after William, Prince of Orange, the name must have sorely troubled the Jacobite clans around, still waiting for their opportunity to return the exiled King James from the House of Stuart to the throne. And if the spirit of the '45 rebellion is alive anywhere today, then it is in the associations of this part of the country with the final flare of the Jacobite cause and its champion, Prince Charles Edward Stuart. The West Highland Museum tells the story and displays fascinating relics of the period.

Right: *Fort William.* Below: *The remains of the fort at Fort William in the 1880s, before its demolition to make way for the railway. (*Royal Commission on Ancient Monuments, Scotland*)*

The signs of industry around the town perhaps surprise some visitors expecting only Highland charm. Aluminium and paper were the main areas of development and both proved sadly vulnerable in recent economic

uncertainties. Given its position historically at the south end of the Caledonian Canal, with good rail links to main population centres further south, convenient sheltered anchorages and the nearness to hydroelectric power schemes, it is hardly surprising that the spread of housing, piers and pipelines below the bulk of Ben Nevis is functional and purpose-

ful, rather than picturesque.

Fort William's fame for tourists lies not only in its situation as a kind of Highland gateway but also in its own nearness to the mightiest of Scotland's mountains. Comparatively recent surveying has fixed the height of Ben Nevis at 4,418 feet – although it was not until 1870 that it was finally declared the highest. From the near vicinity the visitor is best advised to step back, so to speak, to appreciate its height and bulk. The Mallaig road gives splendid distant views, as does the B8004 on the far bank of the Caledonian Canal, starting at Neptune's Staircase. Its size is emphasised as it sweeps up from sea level and inexperienced walkers should attempt the summit by the rough track from Achintee. Stout footwear, warm clothing and a measure of common sense are all advised. Once the summit plateau had a weather observatory, which operated from 1883 to 1904. A hotel on the summit survived till 1915.

Even away from the ancient eroded summit plateau of the Ben, geological history has made its dramatic mark on the scene.

Below: *This series of eight locks near Banavie on the Caledonian Canal is known as 'Neptune's Staircase'*

Above: *The rounded bulk of Ben Nevis ends in steep cliffs on its northern face*

Parallel Roads

Instead of whizzing up to the Commando Memorial beyond the A82/A86 road junction, a worthwhile diversion can be made by taking the A86 eastwards, then driving cautiously up Glen Roy to view the Parallel Roads, clear evidence of spectacular glaciers in the surprisingly recent past. About ten thousand years ago, glaciers covered Lochaber, damming the end of Glen Roy, which filled with waters flowing off the hills beyond. The Parallel Roads are the well-defined shorelines of this huge loch that once filled the valley. As the great glacier in the main valley westward melted, the Glen Roy water level dropped – so, obviously, the highest 'road' is the oldest. The area is now in the care of the Nature Conservancy Council and there is an appropriately sited car park.

While returning to the Great Glen by the A86, it is worth remembering that this main road is a useful escape route eastwards, should the Atlantic south-westerlies be proving particularly moist. Otherwise the bulk of the Monadliath, the great rolling, faceless mountains, northwest of the Cairngorms, are not breached by any through routes until Inverness and the A9. However, the Commando Memorial, only yards from the main road, is the usual stop on the trail. Considerably fewer visitors go down the B8004 nearby, for a very different profile of the Great Glen. The Caledonian Canal before it reaches Loch Lochy is a peaceful winding waterway, and there are barely-discernible parts of a Wade Road to be discovered and the visitor can also detour towards Loch Arkaig.

In spite of intense forestry activity in the Glen Loy and Struan area, Loch Arkaig itself is

Right: *The Commando Monument by Scott Sutherland gives magnificent views of these soldiers' mountainous training grounds.* Below: *Glen Roy's parallel roads*

Left: *Loch Laggan on the road linking the Great Glen with Speyside*

worth a visit. Nearby Achnacarry House (private) was the wartime Command Training Centre headquarters, where over twenty-five thousand men of various nationalities received instruction in the wild country round about. The River Arkaig has picturesque waterfalls and there are more as Loch Arkaig itself is approached through 'The Dark Mile'.

This name refers to the gloomy valley, hung with moss and hemmed in with regimented conifers, which has disappointed travellers for generations – Robert Southey the poet in 1819 commented 'It is not such as this appellation would lead a traveller to expect.' Clearly, the romantic title refers to an earlier age, when there was but a rough track through, some authorities say, ancient dark beeches. Hereabouts is Cameron territory – after the 1745 rebellion, the outlawed Cameron of Clunes took to the woods around to escape the military search parties. The fugitive prince himself sheltered with him for some time. There is a Prince Charlie's cave a little to the north on the wooded slopes and Loch Arkaig itself saw the defeated prince escaping westwards after Culloden along its north bank in April of '46. He was to be hunted for five months until his tortuous wanderings were ended when via the south bank of Arkaig, he reached the coast and a ship for France.

Thus, in fact, it would be wrong to suggest that the vicinity of the Dark Mile is disappointing – quite the reverse – a quintessential highland loch on a single-track

Left: *Loch Arkaig, west of the Great Glen; countryside known by Prince Charles Edward Stuart after the failure of the 1745 rebellion.* Right: *The Well of the Seven Heads recalls a bloody local feud*

peaceful road through wild scenery with its romantic associations of rebellion and clan warfare – and some eerie tales, too.

The waterfall pool by the roadside just before the loch is called the Witch's Cauldron. It got its name after the Camerons were troubled by a sickness amongst their cattle. Suspicion fell on an old woman living near Arkaig's shore – the evil eye gave vets enormous problems in those days. Sure enough, when the clan investigated the woman's house they found a fierce striped cat instead. They attacked it, though it escaped wounded. Following its bloody trail they found it at this waterfall. Closing in to despatch it, suddenly the clansmen saw the wounded beast leap screaming into the air, over the fall and into the dark pool below. As it did so, it changed back to the shape of the crone, thereby confirming their suspicions. Deciding that cattle welfare was more beneficial than charity towards the old woman in feline form, they stoned her to death as she struggled in the water. The cattle's health, natur-

ally, then improved greatly.

Any forays westward are inevitably cul-de-sacs for the motorist. Back on the A82 on Loch Lochyside, the grand sweep of the hillsides are chequered by felling operations, rhododendrons grow over the Fort Augustus railway, soon to become as faint as a Wade Road, and the ancient mausoleum of the Chiefs of Glengarry is on the far bank at the north end of the Loch, visible from the main road.

Above the Laggan Locks, the main road swings over the Laggan bridge, which also swings to allow the passage of vessels on the canal. Loch Quoich was the home of the biggest ever brown trout landed in Britain. It also has a grisly memorial on its bank, by the roadside. This is a monument erected in 1812 to an act of vengeance carried out in 1665. Many stop at the monument, but the tortuous tale it represents is neither easily told nor simply remembered, involving a disputed claim, a rigged accident, two chieftains with a greater or lesser interest in the whole business and a bard whose ear for music seemed

Above: *The Caledonian Canal was originally built in the days of sail, seen in this view of Loch Oich and the ruined Invergarry Castle.* Above left: *Invergarry Castle on the west bank of Loch Oich was burned by the Duke of Cumberland in reprisal after the defeat of the Jacobite forces at Culloden.* Left: *Loch Ness*

to have been exceeded by his thirst for blood.

In 1663 two young members of the Keppoch family were murdered in a dispute concerning rights of succession to the chieftainship of Keppoch. Their mur-

derers, another branch of the MacDonells of Keppoch, claimed it was an accident. Ian Lom, the Keppoch bard, took the case to the chief of Glengarry, who was not inclined to become involved. After two years he eventually persuaded a MacDonald chief in Skye to help avenge the wrongful deed by sending armed men back with the bloodthirsty bard. Ian Lom and his supporters went directly to the murderers' home and slew them. Demonstrating a fine sense of drama Ian then cut their heads off and set off with them over his shoulder to show to the Invergarry chief who had not helped him in the first place. Placing

hygiene before tactfulness, he stopped to wash his hands en route at the well that is now covered by the monument, subsequently placed there by the last chief of Glengarry.

Hurrying on to cheerier places, northwards beyond the road junction (the 'Road to the Isles'), further on than little Loch Oich, Fort Augustus is reached. After the debacle of the 1719 Glenshiel uprising, a nervous government over the border decided that Highland garrisoning should have some priority. The little township of Killichuimen at the south end of Loch Ness found itself occupied and called Fort Augustus.

The site of the fort itself was rebuilt as a Benedictine Abbey, now a boys' school, but Fort Augustus is a picturesque spot, with the bustle of canal locks right in the middle, as well as a nearby Great Glen Heritage Centre. From here on, you can go monster-spotting, all the way to Inverness – and with a choice of routes, though the main road on the west bank probably gives the most frequent glimpses of the water.

Left: *Though pleasure craft are the Caledonian Canal's main users, there is still some commercial traffic, like these fishing boats.* Below far left: *Inside the Benedictine Abbey of Augustus on the site of the inal fort.* Below, left: *Fort gustus Abbey, exterior view.* ight and below: *Details of plans or the original Fort Augustus, built for the government by General Wade to subdue the rebel clans and captured by them during the '45 rebellion.* (Royal Commission on Ancient Monuments, Scotland)

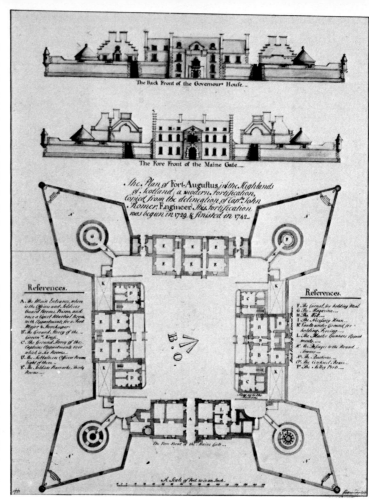

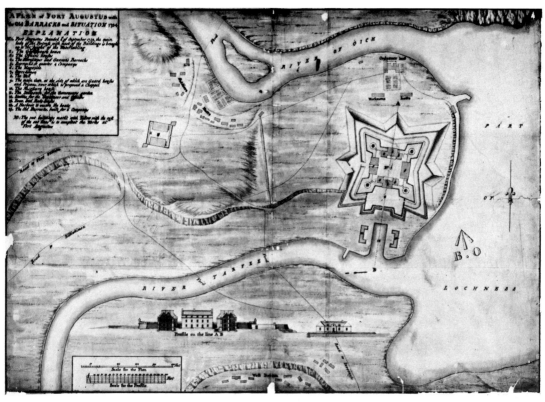

Loch Ness itself is a deep ice-gouged basin, where glacial action succeeded in scouring the rock, already crushed by the faulting, to a depth of nearly 8oo feet – deeper, certainly, than the North Sea. The full length of this massive channel can be appreciated from the roadside just outside Fort Augustus on the B862 – where the shoreline takes the full brunt of the waves from the winter northerlies. The Loch is said never to freeze and to have a locally milder effect on the climate of the immediate environs – with its long, open stretches, dramatic cloudscapes as squalls blow over the circling hills, and steep banks it is a spectacular enough place even

without unknown beasts lurking in its peat-dark waters.

Taking the fast road first, Invermoriston is barely a third of the way up the loch, yet is still twenty-seven miles from Inverness. Nearby in Glenmoriston is a cairn marking the place where one Roderick Mackenzie fell, cut down by a Redcoat's musket-shot as he tried to evade capture – he had been an officer in Prince Charles' Highland army before Culloden. Worse, he knew the Prince to be hiding nearby. As he fell, he cried out 'You have killed your Prince', thereby starting a great deal of confusion and taking some pressure off the pursuit of the real prince, lying close at

Above: Glen Moriston runs west from Invermoriston near the shores of Loch Ness. Below: Mackenzie's Cairn commemorates the death of Roderick Mackenzie who gave his life for his Prince

Above and right: *Urquhart Castle commanded a key position on the roads through the Highlands and was attacked many times.* (Royal Commission on Ancient Monuments, Scotland*)*

hand. Before reaching Drumnadrochit there is another memorial to note – this time to Sir John Cobb who was killed on the Loch in 1952 while attempting to break the world water-speed record. (His boat blew up when it hit some unusual waves at speed – some writers have blamed the elusive monster for producing them.)

A little to the north is the often photographed Urquhart Castle, which has also in its time appeared as backdrop to a few pictures purporting to show . . . something. The castle itself was built and rebuilt on the site of a much earlier bronze age fort. Once one of the largest castles in Scotland, its career as a military stronghold came to an end when it was blown up in 1692 as a consequence of the Jacobite rebellion in 1689.

Beyond Drumnadrochit the hills to the east across the Loch noticeably begin to lose their rugged aspects and a pleasing patchwork of field and woodland encroaches on the wildness. This east bank has its own road, a peaceful but wild and winding route that starts from Fort Augustus and follows the original line surveyed by Wade's men. Little Loch Tarff lies some distance away from the main glen containing Loch Ness itself and is particularly pleasing, while the whole of this southern section between Fort William and Foyers offers fine prospects of Highland scenery, with, in the southern end in particular, random birches rather than regular firs, rolling moorland on the edge of the Monadliath and a sense of remoteness.

Back down on the shores of the great loch, beyond the scattered community of Foyers, Inverfarigaig has a Forestry Commission centre and Farigaig forest trails – then the road alternates every few yards between double and single tracks with plenty of opportunity to stop and scan the loch. Dores marks, at last, the end of Loch Ness and the scenery quickly loses its Highland air for a cooler, saltier flavour – Inverness and the sea.

At the end of the Great Glen, Inverness has a 'gateway' feel to it, bustling with traffic, tidy and geared to the visitor. If it has a Highland flavour, then it is well-diluted by an east-coast briskness. Yet it has the best of several worlds. The rich farmlands of the sheltered Moray coast are only a little way eastwards, while in the other direction lies the bulk of the north-west Highlands. It is a natural route centre, not just up the Great Glen, but by the improved A9.

It has seen its share of troubled times. In 1411 the town was sacked by the Lord of the Isles. In 1428, James I held a parliament there to express his displeasure at the constant warring of his northern subjects. To make his point,

he then imprisoned most of the chiefs who attended and hung a few to emphasise his views. Held in custody was one Alexander, son of the Lord of the Isles, who promptly matched his father's exploit some years before, demon-strating how he felt about the king's mercy by burning the town again as soon as he was released.

Above: *General Wade's military road of 1726 runs along the south shore of Loch Tarff. Today's B862 covers it in places, but in the vicinity of Loch Tarff it is worth looking out for the faint signs of the original route where it deviates from the modern road. Loch Tarff itself is a peaceful and unspoilt spot*

In 1746, just before Culloden (which lies only five miles eastward), the Jacobite army captured Inverness and Prince Charles ordered the destruction of its fort. Because of this violent history, most of Inverness is comparatively recent – Macbeth's Castle has long vanished and the impressive County Offices (1840) stand in for more ancient fortifications. However, Abertarff House, the town house of Lord Lovat, dates from 1593, and the Museum and Art Gallery has an impressive collection of artefacts of Highland folk life. And the town has a splendid range of shopping, accommodation, recreational facilities – ideal for visitors starting, or ending, their tour of the Great Glen.

Right: Aspects of Culloden battlefield where the National Trust for Scotland are currently restoring the site to resemble the moor as it was in 1746. Below: *the Victorian Inverness Castle*

Road, Rail & Waterways in the Great Glen

In the comfort and security of London, George I in 1724 received a complaining note from Simon Fraser, Lord Lovat, from his northern home near the Great Glen. He complained that the Highlands were 'very mountainous and almost inaccessible to any but the inhabitants thereof' and that they 'remain to this day much less civilised than other parts of Scotland'. The authorities recognised the urgency in its tone – it hinted of continuing unrest. By this time Fort William had its barracks, the uprisings of 1715 and 1719 were over – and the government were hoping that the Jacobite cause would not surface again. (This was the name given to supporters of the House of Stuart who wished to overthrow the Hanoverian monarchy.)

The King sent Major-General George Wade north to investigate – and was duly alarmed at his 1724 reports which spoke of ten thousand government supporters – but twelve thousand who would support a rebellion. The result was another Disarming Act and urgent plans to put a military craft on Loch Ness, repair Fort William and build new forts at Fort Augustus and Inverness. Just as important, Wade was given a free hand to improve communications between these fortified sites. He realised that 'foreign' troops unused to rough country and long marches could not move around this unruly territory quickly.

Above right: *Today's Highland Cattle are bigger and heavier beasts than the original black cattle found in the north of Scotland.* Right: *The Caledonian Canal at Dochgarroch, close to Inverness*

Left: *General Wade by Van Deist* (National Galleries of Scotland, Edinburgh). *General Wade's wide remit of observation and control in the rebellious Highlands included road building on his own suggestion. Wade embarked on this new venture in 1726 with 500 men as his road-building squad.* Above: *The Pass of Inverfarigaig.* Below: *Another view of the original Fort Augustus*

By 1726 the first road was complete, running from Inverness to Fort Augustus and taking a route somewhat inland from the lochside. Visitors can follow parts of it today, on the high moorland to the east of Loch Ness. This exposed route was quickly super-seded by a road on the lochside itself, with sections blasted out of steep rock above Inverfarigaig. (It is curious that Nessie failed to show any interest, when the 1930s new roadmaking disturbances are so often given as the reason she stirred from the depths in this century – clearly Wade's men lacked the proper tourist guides.) Wade's Bridge itself at Inver-farigaig is still visible, upstream from and dwarfed by the present one – though crumbling fast. Any visitor taking time to stop at the Farigaig Forest Walks can obtain a fine view of it from the parapet of the main road.

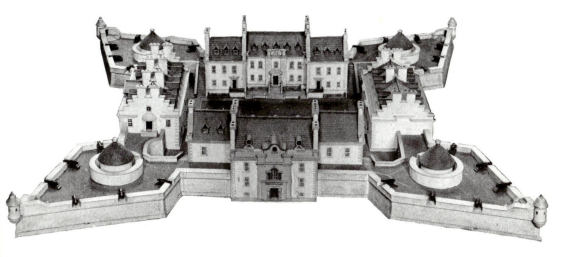

But the finest bridge lies a little to the south – at Whitebridge, after the 1726 and 1732 roads have joined. Look out for the typical raised banking just before Whitebridge itself, though more easily appreciated is the fine hump-backed bridge with its informative notice by the Inverness Field Club, a few yards upstream from the present. Beyond, a straight road rolls over the moorland and it is easy to imagine the companies of 'highwaymen' toiling in the fickle sunlight of a northern spring. The Fort Augustus/Inverness section allows the motorist easiest access to a Wade Road that has not been made utterly unrecognisable by subsequent rebuilding and realignment. There are enough clues remaining to make exploration

and rediscovery rewarding.

However, the Fort Augustus/Fort William section also occupied Wade's attention and to this day a few sections of the road can be found – it takes the south side of Loch Oich, for example, whereas the modern route leaves it for the opposite bank. Both the A82 and the disused Fort Augustus railway have obliterated it in stretches, but an O.S. map will show where the visitor should hunt. For example, not far from the Commando Memorial at Spean Bridge the old highway crosses the B8004, heading for what was once the spectacular Highbridge over the River Spean. It is worth pausing on the public road to find this section – look for a track with a gate across it, going downhill towards the river, one mile west of

Above: *The now ruined Highbridge was built in 1736, after the Inverness–Fort William road was completed. It once spanned the River Spean.* Top right: *The remains of Telford's bridge at Invermoriston represents a later phase of road building.* Right: *Whitebridge, one of the most attractive of Wade's works. (Royal Commission on Ancient Monuments, Scotland)*

the Memorial. Again, the visitor must try to imagine the days when this narrow track was considered an improvement; when the mountains looming beyond must have seemed very unfriendly to a road-building company of men, confident in their arms for protection, but no doubt a little uncomfortable at the rumours of wild clansmen still at odds with the

monarch in distant London.

It is significant that major sections of Wade's Great Glen roads are still in use by the heavy traffic of today – though widened and much altered. One last road out of the glen was his most spectacular, but is much less well known – hardly surprising, as it crosses rough mountainous territory at around two-and-a-half thousand feet. The road through the Corrieyairack Pass was intended to connect Fort Augustus and the Great Glen with Dalwhinnie and the eastern Central Highlands – a function which in modern times was taken over by the A86 Laggan road, itself built as part of Telford's programme nearly a century later. Now the hairpins and high moorland are the province of hillwalkers and the 'Hydro Board' – winter snows overcame any possibility of development into a main arterial route.

Thus the military roads were first to open up the lands of the clans. But by the beginning of the nineteenth century, politicians far to the south had gradually been made aware of the intense economic problems of 'North Britain'. Emigration was already under way, over-population was playing its part – an emptying, broken, sheep-grazed land was resulting, with a high share of absentee landlords. Development of fishing stocks on the west coast was only one solution proposed and to this end, a waterway was needed to join the coasts, removing the danger of the stormy northern coast for civilian and naval craft, too.

Telford was the engineer of the Caledonian Canal, as well as being involved in a major road-building programme, several decades after Wade. On receiving the engineer's surveys, the government acted quickly – it had dawned on the authorities that emigration would shortly affect the supply of Scots for the British army and navy. The canal, with its construction and quarrying works, would provide regular employment. Rather ironically, early work on the canal itself was badly affected by the activities of the press gang. Other complications Telford found in plenty. Local skills were hard enough to

Below: *Glen Spean near Roy Bridge.* Right: *Wade's route from Dalwhinnie to Fort Augustus went over the Corrieyairack Pass at 2,500 ft. Though completed in 1732, the route fell into disuse – ultimately defeated by the severity of the Scottish winters at these high levels. This view shows the road dropping towards Fort Augustus, visible on the left of the picture*

find, local materials even worse. Stone eventually came in by sea from the Cumbraes on the Clyde, bricks came from Liverpool, some wood was available locally for housing – but oak for the lock gates came from the Baltic. Local landowners, Glengarry and Lochiel, bargained for good prices for their own timber – and the burden of organisation fell on John Telford at the Corpach end.

The early years of the project involved not just the southern section, but also the building of the basin at Inverness and the dredging of Loch Oich. By 1818 vessels could enter Loch Ness from the north and finally in 1822 the construction was completed – though only to a depth of twelve feet and not twenty feet as originally intended for naval vessels. But industrial developments were to overtake it. Vessels became too large, the railways arrived and road communications improved, so that the canal never really fulfilled its promise. It is still used by some commercial fishing vessels, but it is pleasure craft you will see most frequently.

The communications of the Great Glen have one sad tailpiece. By the 1890s, Fort William had its railway, the West Highland, and it was from Spean Bridge that the Invergarry and Fort Augustus Railway was planned to branch northwards up the Great Glen. There was talk of a fast new line to Inverness – a prospect which the Highland Railway, already established there, viewed with some alarm. The little I & FA took ground for a double track, engineered expensive viaducts, cuttings and tunnellings – they even built a pier and pier station on Loch Ness. To this day, at the top end of the Fort

Right: *Fort Augustus at the south end of Loch Ness. The Caledonian Canal locks are in the top right of the picture with the piers of the abandoned railway on the far right*

Augustus lochs, there are still the remains of the extravagant bridge that led by a costly embankment the short distance to the waterside. It opened in 1903. The Highland Railway cunningly offered to work the railway – to make sure it never got to Inverness via the efforts of their rivals, the North British, whose tracks the I & FA left at Spean Bridge. To make doubly sure, the Highland then shortened its own main line to Inverness by thirty miles – effectively stranding the little railway with no hope of ever heading further up the glen. By

1907 the Fort Augustus pier station was closed. Next, the Highland withdrew its support. The North British reluctantly moved in on unfavourable terms but in turn abandoned the unprofitable line by 1911.

Protests by locals, campaigns and questions in Parliament followed – a common enough situation some half-century later when railways were being decimated country-wide – but here in the Great Glen was the first ever protest about a railway closure. It succeeded in its aim. The line survived as an unprofitable

Above: *A straight course over the moors between Loch Ness and the Monadliath – the B862 on the line of Wade's road*

branch from its reopening in 1913 till 1933, when passenger services ceased. It closed to all traffic in 1946. Imagine the magnificence of the scenery, viewed from its coaches, had the line got through to its destination. Now the rhododendrons grow on the embankments and its track-bed is gradually disappearing, like Wade's roads before it.

the evidence of the sixties and early seventies had suggested that the phenomenon was extremely difficult to photograph on the surface. Consequently, forays were made underwater. The subject matter photographed by Dr Rines in June 1975, forty feet down in the peat-fogged darkness has been decidedly controversial – the well-known image of the 'gargoyle head' decidedly disturb-

Top: *Drumnadrochit's Loch Ness Monster Exhibition Centre makes essential visiting – the evidence is presented for visitors to make up their own minds*. Above: *An optimist's model – or the real thing?* Right: *The countryside around Drumnadrochit, west of Loch Ness. Note the farming on the valley floor, the forestry on the upper slopes and the bare moors above*

The Elusive Monster of Loch Ness

Mention Loch Ness to the most casual of tourists and the conversation turns to monsters. What started as a news item in a quiet week on the local newspaper in the thirties, is now a major attraction and prop for the local tourism industry. The phenomenon was under way by 1933, suitably bolstered by retrospective sightings, suddenly recalled. St Columba was brought in as a respectable witness – for the saint frightened a beast in the River Ness as it was about to attack a swimmer – all this in AD 565.

Not surprisingly, hoaxers were quickly on the scene and have lurked around ever since, making footprints or building their own monsters. The Church, too, was not altogether approving of this fuss. A minister of the Free Church of Fort Augustus wrote nearly fifty years ago: 'the word "monster" is really not applicable to the Loch Ness animal, but is truly applicable to those who deliberately sin against the light of law and revelation.' He was referring to those visitors from other parts who came to view the animal on a Sunday.

By 1934 the first head and neck photograph had been taken, followed by humps in the fifties, but most pictures lacked a scale, making logs, rocks, floating vegetation, swimming red deer, otters, cormorants, boats' wakes,

Top right: Urquhart Castle, favourite vantage point for monster spotters. Right: On any other loch, an everyday occurrence – boats' wakes crossing in still water conditions – goes unremarked. On Loch Ness the wave patterns become a monster!

mirages, even labrador dogs retrieving sticks all equally plausible interpretations. But still the legend wouldn't go away.

In 1957, Constance Whyte published *More than a Legend*, the prototypical handbook for the followers of the monster cult. This in turn inspired a new generation of hunters in the sixties. Dubious cine-film was shot, a few more

stills were taken, new books appeared and, enraged by the continuing attention focussed on Loch Ness, a beast in Loch Morar attacked a rowing boat. By the early seventies, there were a lot of cameras overlooking the loch.

But curiously, the numbers of sightings seemed in inverse proportion to the number of lenses trained on the surface. Overall,

Above: *A monster classic, the famous 'surgeon's photograph' of 1934. Could it be the monster's head or a diving otter's tail?*
Below: *P. A. MacNab's 1955* telephoto picture has Urquhart Castle for scale. Is it just unusual wave patterns or a bulky creature cruising just below the surface? *(Daily Express)*

ing, but the scientific establishment still demanded more than vague shapes.

The eighties have seen a more cautious approach to the investigation of the phenomenon. The Loch Ness and Morar project has established, through investigation of the loch floor, that a stable environment exists at these extreme depths. There is evidence of fish stocks – thus a large organism could survive. Sonar tracking has recorded significant single targets, not easily explained as fish shoals. By the mid-eighties, the best evidence lies in these recordings, available for the visitors to inspect at the Loch Ness monster Official Exhibition at Drumnadrochit. On display, too, is the visual evidence through the years and the testimonies of many reliable witnesses. The whole exhibition is a thought-provoking experience.

The peculiarly Scottish legal verdict of 'unproven' must at present rest on the case for the beast. Perhaps we 'need' a monster – the fear of the unknown, the excitement of some vast denizen under the noses of the establishment, the romance of dark unexplored landscapes of the imagination. Thus we welcome evidence that is positive – reliable witnesses, unexplained photographs – and reject other explanations – such as the not uncommon phenomenon for large bodies of water in still conditions to give rise to mirage conditions – shimmering air masses that can distort everyday objects.

Loch Ness certainly has a phenomenon, an intermittent series of mainly visual disturbances which are so far unexplained in geological, meteorological or zoological terms. It forms a unique part of the atmosphere of the Great Glen.

Text by Gilbert J. Summers
ISBN 0–7117–0262–4
© 1986 Jarrold Colour Publications
Printed in Great Britain by Jarrold & Sons Ltd, Norwich. 186.